SHE KNOWS
HER WORTH

Empowerment through Self-Respect and Confidence

HANNA OLIVAS

ALONG WITH 8 INSPIRING AUTHORS

ISBN: 978-1-966798-49-1

TABLE OF CONTENTS

INTRODUCTION

Every woman has an incredible story of discovering her worth—an unfolding journey of self-realization, growth, and empowerment. In a world that often asks women to shrink or doubt themselves, it can be easy to lose sight of just how valuable and powerful we truly are. *She Knows Her Worth: Empowerment through Self-Respect and Confidence* is here to guide you on this life-changing journey, helping you reconnect with your own strength, beauty, and potential.

Inside this book, you'll hear from women who, just like you, have faced the doubts, insecurities, and challenges that come with finding self-worth. Their stories are not just about surviving these struggles—they are about embracing them and rising stronger. They've learned to silence the harsh inner critic, to respect their own needs, and to walk with heads held high. These voices, full of honesty and warmth, offer you the wisdom and encouragement of a trusted friend.

But this book doesn't stop at inspiring stories. It's a practical guide filled with actionable tips and strategies to help you live out your worth every day. You'll discover simple, effective ways to quiet your inner doubts, establish healthy boundaries, and celebrate your victories—no matter how small. You'll also learn how to cultivate a mindset that empowers you to see yourself as you truly are: worthy of love, respect, and success.

Whether you're just beginning your journey toward self-discovery or you've been walking it for some time, *She Knows Her Worth* will help you take the next step with confidence. This isn't just about learning tips—it's about a shift in perspective, a commitment to treating yourself with the same love and respect you give to others.

Get ready to transform your inner dialogue, elevate your self-respect, and embrace your power. The road to confidence starts here—and you've already taken the first step by picking up this book.

Welcome to your journey. You are worthy.

Hanna Olivas

Founder and CEO of SHE RISES STUDIOS

https://www.linkedin.com/company/she-rises-studios/
https://www.facebook.com/sherisesstudios
https://www.instagram.com/sherisesstudios_llc/
www.SheRisesStudios.com

Author, Speaker, and Founder. Hanna was born and raised in Las Vegas, Nevada, and has paved her way to becoming one of the most influential women of 2022. Hanna is the co-founder of She Rises Studios and the founder of the Brave & Beautiful Blood Cancer Foundation. Her journey started in 2017 when she was first diagnosed with Multiple Myeloma, an incurable blood cancer. Now more than ever, her focus is to empower other women to become leaders because The Future is Female. She is currently traveling and speaking publicly to women to educate them on entrepreneurship, leadership, and owning the female power within.

She Knows Her Worth:
A Journey of Rediscovery

By Hanna Olivas

There's a moment in every woman's life when she asks herself, *Am I enough?* It's a question that cuts to the core, that challenges everything we've been told to believe about ourselves, and it's one that too many of us struggle with. For so long, we're taught to look outside of ourselves for validation—to measure our worth by what others think of us, by how much we achieve, or by how perfectly we can fit into the molds the world sets for us. But here's the truth I've come to understand after years of searching, struggling, and finally, rising: "You don't need the world to tell you your worth—you already hold that power within you."

My journey to understanding my own worth hasn't been a straight line. Like so many women, I've spent years questioning whether I was enough—enough to lead, enough to dream, enough to succeed. I've walked through dark valleys of doubt, where it felt like the weight of the world's expectations was pressing down on me, and I wasn't sure if I could carry it any longer. I've had moments when I let other people's opinions define me, moments when I dimmed my light because I thought that's what I needed to do to be accepted.

But what I've learned, through the struggles and the victories, is this: "Your worth is not something you earn; it's something you already possess." It's taken me a long time to get to a place where I truly believe that, where I not only know it in my head but feel it in my heart. And now, as I stand on the other side of that journey, I can see how powerful it is to claim your worth, to own it fully and unapologetically.

For women, the path to knowing our worth is often fraught with challenges. Society doesn't always make it easy for us to see our own value. We're told that we need to be smaller, quieter, less of everything in order to be worthy. We're conditioned to believe that our worth is tied to how much we do for others, to how perfectly we perform in all the roles we play—mother, daughter, wife, entrepreneur, friend. But here's what I want every woman to know: "Your worth isn't measured by what you do; it's measured by who you are."

It wasn't until I hit a low point in my life—where everything I thought I knew about myself seemed to crumble—that I began to rediscover my own worth. I was overwhelmed, stretched too thin, and feeling like no matter how much I gave, it was never enough. I was trying to do it all, to be everything to everyone, and in the process, I lost sight of myself. That's when I realized something had to change. "When you lose yourself in trying to meet everyone else's expectations, you forget the most important thing—you are worthy just as you are."

There's a mantra that has carried me through some of my darkest moments: "I am enough, just as I am." It's simple, but it's also one of the most profound truths I've come to understand. There were days when I had to repeat it to myself over and over again until I began to believe it. And slowly, I started to let go of the need for external validation. I stopped looking to others to tell me that I was worthy. Instead, I began to look within. I realized that my worth wasn't something anyone else could give me or take away from me. It was mine, inherent, unshakable, and true.

One of the hardest lessons I've learned is that "worthiness isn't about perfection; it's about authenticity." For so long, I thought that in order to be worthy, I had to have it all together—I had to be flawless. But the truth is, our worth is found in our imperfections. It's found in our vulnerability, in our willingness to show up as we are, even when we're messy, even when we're still figuring things out. Knowing your worth means embracing all of yourself, the light and the dark, the successes and the failures.

For me, the journey to knowing my worth also meant learning to trust myself again. Trusting that I had the answers within me, that I didn't need to look to others to tell me what I should do or who I should be. It was about reclaiming my own voice and trusting that it was enough. "When you trust yourself, you reclaim your power." That's a truth that took me years to fully grasp. But once I did, it was like a weight lifted off my shoulders. I no longer needed to prove myself to anyone. I knew my worth, and that was all that mattered.

Another mantra that has become a cornerstone in my life is this: "I am worthy of love, of joy, of success, of everything my heart desires." There were times when I didn't believe that. There were times when I thought I had to settle, that I didn't deserve the things I truly wanted. But what I've come to realize is that "worthiness is not about what you've done; it's about who you are." And who I am—who you are—is inherently worthy of everything good.

One of the things that holds so many of us back from truly knowing our worth is the fear of being "too much" or "not enough." I've felt that fear deeply. I've wondered if I was too loud, too bold, too ambitious. I've also wondered if I was smart enough, talented enough, or worthy enough to chase my dreams. But here's the truth I've come to embrace: "You are never too much, and you are always enough." You don't have to shrink yourself to fit into anyone else's idea of who you should be. You don't have to dull your light to make others comfortable. Your worth is not up for negotiation.

I believe that every woman has a light inside of her—a unique brilliance that is hers and hers alone. But too often, we're taught to hide that light, to keep it small, to stay in the background. But knowing your worth means stepping into your light, fully and unapologetically. "You are allowed to take up space. You are allowed to shine." Once I realized that, my entire perspective shifted. I no longer felt like I had to hold back. I knew that my worth was not contingent on anyone else's approval.

Of course, the journey to knowing your worth isn't always easy. There will be times when doubt creeps in, when the world tries to tell you that you're not enough, or when you question your own value. But in those moments, I remind myself of this: "Worthiness isn't something you earn—it's something you remember." It's a truth that lives inside of you, even when you forget it, even when the world tries to make you doubt it. And once you reconnect with that truth, once you truly know your worth, nothing can take it away.

Helping other women rediscover their own worth has become one of the most meaningful parts of my journey. I see so many women struggling with the same doubts and fears I once had, and I want them to know that they are not alone. "Every woman is worthy of the life she dreams of, the love she deserves, and the success she's capable of." Sometimes, we just need someone to remind us of that, to reflect back the light we've always carried.

One of the most profound realizations I've had is that "knowing your worth isn't just about you—it's about the impact you have on others." When you know your worth, you show up differently in the world. You carry yourself with confidence, you set boundaries that protect your peace, and you inspire others to do the same. Your glow becomes contagious. Other women see you standing in your power, and they realize that they, too, are worthy of standing in theirs.

I've made it my mission to help women reconnect with their own worth because I know how life-changing it can be. When you know your worth, everything shifts. You stop settling for less than you deserve. You stop questioning whether you're capable. You stop playing small. "When a woman knows her worth, she becomes unstoppable." That's the power of worthiness—it opens doors, it breaks barriers, and it transforms lives.

One of the things I've learned is that knowing your worth doesn't mean you'll never doubt yourself again. There will still be moments of insecurity, moments when you question whether you're on the right path. But the difference is, when you know your worth, those moments don't define you. You have an unshakable foundation to fall back on. You know, deep down, that no matter what happens, you are enough. "Doubt may visit, but it will never take root when you know your worth."

The journey to knowing your worth is a lifelong one. It's not something you arrive at and then never have to think about again. It's something you cultivate, something you practice every day. It's about choosing, over and over again, to believe in your own value, even when it feels hard. "Worthiness is a daily practice of choosing yourself." And the more you choose yourself, the stronger that belief becomes.

To every woman reading this, I want you to know that you are worthy. Not because of what you've accomplished, not because of how much you give to others, but because of who you are. You are worthy of love, of joy, of success, and of every dream you hold in your heart.

"Your worth is not something you have to prove; it's something you embrace." You don't need the world to validate you, and you don't need to measure yourself by anyone else's standards. Your worth is already within you—strong, unshakable, and undeniable.

As you move forward on your journey, remember this: "You are worthy simply because you exist." You don't need to do more, be more, or give more to deserve the life you dream of. It's already yours. The moment you claim your worth, the moment you believe in it fully, is the moment everything begins to change.

You will rise, not because the world gives you permission, but because you give yourself permission. You will rise because you know, deep down, that you are worthy of everything life has to offer. And when you rise, you will inspire others to rise with you.

So, here's to you—the woman who knows her worth, the woman who is reclaiming her power, the woman who will no longer settle for anything less than she deserves. Your journey is just beginning, and the world is waiting for your light to shine.

Remember, "She knows her worth, and because of that, she is unstoppable."

Dorcas Bosede Frank

Founder & CEO of Virtue Series Publishers LTD / Virtue Montessori Model School/ Dorcas Virtue Foundation.
Best selling Author, Serial Entrepreneur, public speaker, educational consultant, transformation and Business coach and a Woman Financial Empowerment Advocate.

https://www.linkedin.com/in/dorcas-frank-611783162
https://www.instagram.com/dorcas_bosede_frank/
https://www.facebook.com/Dorcasbosedefrank/
https://dorcasbosedefrank.com/

Dorcas Bosede Frank is a seasoned and an award winning thought leader, educator, curriculum expert, and entrepreneur with over 35 years of experience. She is the founder of Virtue Montessori Model School, renowned for raising confident, morally upright children equipped with 21st-century skills through innovative teaching methods, including STEAM education, entrepreneurship, and practical learning. As CEO of Virtue Series Publishers Ltd, Dorcas has authored and published over 70 widely acclaimed educational books. She is also an empowerment coach, inspiring women and youth to achieve financial independence and personal growth. Her NGO focuses on empowering women, youth, and children, addressing societal challenges in northern Nigeria.

A proud mother of seven and a former soldier's wife, Dorcas uses her resilience and life experiences to inspire others. She is committed to writing transformational books, creating impactful courses, and becoming a global leader in education and women empowerment.

Rising from the Ashes:
A Journey of Self-Worth and Empowerment

By Dorcas Bosede Frank

Life, for me, began as a whirlwind of trials and uncertainties. Losing my father in a car crash at just six years old shattered the foundation of my world. Thrown into the care of relatives unwilling to invest in my education, I found myself struggling to hold onto the hope of a brighter future. Though academically gifted, I was consumed by shyness and timidity, particularly around men, having spent my formative years in an all-girls school.

The turning point began with a heartbreak—my first failed relationship. Set up and lied about, I felt betrayed and humiliated. In my quest to escape the pain, I stumbled into another relationship with a young man from a wealthy family. What began as a flicker of hope soon turned into a storm when I discovered I was pregnant. The young man, under the influence of an associate who despised me, refused to take responsibility. His rejection was rooted in a disdain for my social class.

I will never forget the sting of that rejection. But instead of letting it break me, I made a resolute decision: to rise above my mistakes and prove my worth—not just to them but to myself.

"I will work on myself until they regret losing me," I vowed. "They will see me on TV one day and realize I was the wife they let slip away."

I promised myself I would not be a burden to my widowed mother, who was already struggling to raise my siblings. I would not allow my child to grow up despised or unloved because of my circumstances.

With this resolve, I began my journey. I took up menial jobs to prepare for my baby's arrival, refusing to place the weight of my mistakes on my mother's already strained shoulders. A year after giving birth, I secured admission to a Federal College of Education – An advanced Teacher Training Institution. As a single parent, I excelled academically, even surpassing many of my peers, all while balancing the demands of motherhood and work. I sold goods, attended promotional events, and offered home lessons to fund my education and care for my child.

After graduating, I became a teacher, combining my job with neighborhood grocery sales and tutoring. My desire to grow and learn became insatiable. I attended seminars and workshops on women's development, success, and wealth creation, which ignited a passion in me for personal and financial empowerment.

Through relentless determination, I returned to the university for further studies, funding my education through selling recharge cards and home lessons. These experiences taught me resilience and discipline, shaping me into a woman determined to change her narrative.

Today, I am proud to stand as a living testament to what self-respect, determination, and confidence can achieve. I am happily married to Frank, a supportive partner who shares my vision for life. Together, we have built a thriving life, anchored on mutual respect and shared goals. I am the founder of Virtue Montessori Model School, Virtue Series Publishers Ltd, and the Dorcas Virtue Foundation, alongside several coaching services.

My journey taught me to turn pain into purpose. The trials I faced as a young mother gave me the drive to empower women to reinvent themselves, find purpose, and gain financial independence. I teach them that everyone has the capacity for greatness—but they must take responsibility and action to achieve it.

The lasting effects of my turning point are woven into every aspect of my life. My past no longer defines me; instead, it fuels my passion to inspire others. Women who feel trapped in their circumstances need to hear this: You have the power to rewrite your story. You are not defined by where you come from or the mistakes you've made but by the decisions you make moving forward.

I stand today as a voice for women who have been silenced by shame, fear, or societal expectations. I remind them that self-respect and confidence are the cornerstones of empowerment. I know my worth, and I will continue to teach others to discover theirs.

This is my story, a story of rising from the ashes to become a beacon of hope and empowerment for others. It is proof that no matter how dark your beginnings, you can always find the light within yourself to shine.

Rachel Krall

Uprooted Consulting, LLC
Success & Wellbeing Coach

https://uprootmylife.com/

Rachel is a Success + Wellbeing Coach, Master Practitioner of NLP, and yoga teacher dedicated to helping high-achieving women find peace, purpose, and aligned, sustainable success. With a unique blend of mindset work, nervous system regulation, and spiritual wisdom, she guides women to reconnect with themselves, release burnout, and redefine success on their own terms. Through her signature framework, Rachel empowers clients to rise from overwhelm into clarity, confidence, and conviction—without sacrificing their wellbeing.

Finding Confidence Beyond Approval

By Rachel Krall

We all have it; that moment stored in our memory, when we first learned that confidence is fragile. For me, it was my freshman year of high school. It was the week of Homecoming—Spirit Week. Each day was a themed day, and the first day—the day I will never forget—was 80s day. I loved dressing up, so I couldn't wait to go ALL IN! I found a bright-colored, off-the-shoulder shirt from my mom's closet, paired it with some leggings, scrunchy socks, and a huge belt, and made my naturally curly hair as big as it could be. I looked like a character from *Saved by the Bell*. I couldn't wait to see what others were wearing.

I walked into the lobby, and some of my friends saw me and started laughing and shaking their heads. I blew it off. I was a theater girl. Dress-up was my thing. I committed to the part, and I was owning it. But then, my prom date—a junior—and the person whose approval I wanted most saw me, laughed, and walked away like he didn't even know me. Then, others followed his lead, pointing and laughing. Their gazes snapped at me like a photo, dissecting me pixel by pixel. I watched as their judgment sharpened with each flaw they uncovered. I guess I should be grateful there were no camera phones back then. It took everything in me not to run to the nurse and pretend I was sick (not that my parents played that game, anyway). I suffered through the day, wishing I was invisible. It goes without saying that I did not dress up any other day that week, or off-stage again for a very long time.

Since then, I've seen similar scenes played out in movies where the main character keeps her cool by making a quotable comeback or even starting a new trend. I wish that was the case for me, but it wasn't. It broke my confidence and stored a new core memory that I would never forget. That moment created a belief that would take me years to work through, a belief that other people's opinions matter more than my own.

As I grew older, confidence became a trait I sought after. I wanted to be perceived as a confident person, so I played the part like the actor I was in high school. I put on the types of clothes that confident people would wear. I studied movies and shows and styled myself like the confident women I admired. I chased achievements, titles, and identities that confident people held. I worked hard at it. I was described as "confident" by others. I worked hard to prove myself to the world and myself. I learned tools to act confident and feel confident. At this point in my life, I believed I was confident.

But everything changed when I became a mom. Mom groups were like high school all over again. The first one my son and I attended was located at a public park. I brought my son to the playground, and he began climbing on a rope ladder when a "concerned" mom came over to introduce herself. "You're OK with him climbing that by himself?" she asked. I nodded. "He loves climbing." After several minutes, he ran over to me for his sippy cup. Then the mom looked at me and shockingly said, "Is that a character t-shirt?" I responded, confused. "Uh, yes. Monsters Inc." She then looked me straight in the face and said, "I would never let my child wear character clothes." Later, I overheard her calling my son's shirt "tacky."

I immediately flashed back to 80s Spirit Day. I felt scared and angry that a grown woman would judge my child for wearing a shirt with a character that he loves. If he were old enough to understand her, would he be embarrassed to wear this shirt? Would he dull himself like I did after 80s day? I would do everything I could from that day forward to set him up to have confidence in himself. Not in approval from me. Not in approval from his teachers. Not in approval from his friends. But trust in his own abilities, decisions, and worth.

I refused to let history repeat itself. I knew firsthand how quickly a single comment could plant the seed of self-doubt. I wanted something different for my son. I wanted him to stand firm in his choices, to wear what he loved without hesitation, to move through the world with the unshakable belief that his worth was not up for debate. Confidence, I realized, wasn't about shielding him from judgment. It was about equipping him with the resources to stand tall in spite of it.

As humans, we are wired to seek external validation; it's part of how we navigate belonging. In a world where likes and follows feel like a measure of worth, and approval has become the currency of our time, it's easy to believe confidence comes from being chosen.

But true confidence isn't about whether others approve of your outfit, your parenting, or your choices. It's about trusting yourself enough to make decisions for you and being resilient enough to accept when you get it wrong. Learn from it. You deserve the right to change your mind. We are ever-evolving, ever-changing, ever-becoming. Confidence isn't about getting it right every time. It's about choosing yourself—again and again and again.

Terrie Green

A Grateful Journey

By Terrie Green

How I got started on my crazy journey. I was blessed at a young age with the gift of baking. At the age of nine I entered my cookies in the local county fair through the 4-H program. Winning ribbons on my cookies really inspired me to continue my childhood baking.

However, I never in a million years did I think I would be opening my own bakery. I've always had an entrepreneurial spirit. My journey really began in the eighties, the fashion industry. After graduating from Chico State University with a Bachelor of Science, I moved to New York City to pursue my fashion career. I was fortunate to get a job with Macy's in New York, Manhattan. I worked as a department manager in one of the designer fashion departments. After about a year, I realized I could not afford to live in Manhattan on the management salary I received and came back to California to take a position with Macy's in Sacramento as the Housewares department manager, where I thrived. I realized how much I always loved being in the kitchen.

As it turned out I had a supervisor that was sexually harassing me. I tried to talk with the personnel department about the matter. This was in the mid-eighties, and there was no such thing as a sexual harassment policy. The harassment continued until it jeopardized my career. I felt like I had no other choice then to get an attorney and press charges. Fortunately, the case was in my favor, and we settled out of court! The main reason I felt I had to take this action was to help other women who were dealing with the same problem I was. This was a male-dominated industry, and they were using their positions to coerce women who wanted to move up in the company.

I have worked very hard to advance my professional career in the fashion industry, as it has been a dream of mine since I was a little girl. The good news was Macy's put in place the first sexual harassment policy! Bad news, my file was closed. So, all the hard work I put into my dream career meant doors were now closed to me. I would be viewed as a troublemaker.

What was to follow changed my course for life in a wonderful way.

The only job I could find quickly was at a new café that moved in my area from LA. I jumped at the opportunity. Because of my resume, they hired me on the spot to do the buying for their small gift shop. Before long, I was managing the café and gift shop. This is where my baking career started. The baked goods the café was selling were from a bakery in San Francisco, and I felt I baked a better product, specifically shortbread. So, I asked if I could attempt to sell it in the café. They eagerly agreed!

The shortbread was so well received that I started baking other products. After my shift was done, I would bake at night in my cute little pink 18" gas oven at home. I would then take them to work the next morning...and THAT is where my career in food service began! I love to bake. I love being in the kitchen. I love the wonderful response from the customers.

My food service journey has been amazing. I've had the pleasure of doing wholesale baking, retail baking, as well as catering. All the while growing my business and having and raising three amazing children as a single mom! I was always able to have my children with me and that in itself was a blessing. I opened my first brick-and-mortar bakery when my oldest daughter Tara was only one month old on Valentine's Day. I opened my second location when my son Kinsey was three months old, and two years later, I had my third baby Nika!

After several years of growing the business, getting up to bake at 3:00 a.m., and all the pressures that go along with staffing, I made the hard decision to sell the business and move to the country. This way, I could slow the pace. I kept a few wholesale accounts and homeschooled my kids so I would be more present in their lives. We had a blast. But after about five years, I was itching to work again. I chose to become a real estate agent. That way, I could still be with the kids due to the flexibility of work hours in the industry. I worked very, very hard, and by the end of the first year, I had earned Rookie of the Year. I was determined to cut the five-year learning curve down to one year. I did. Every year, I was awarded one of the Top Producers in the industry. I also helped open two award-winning real estate company offices. What a ride it was, but always in the back of my mind, I missed baking and was hoping to open another bakery.

Well, the opportunity came. My kids were older and able to help when I found the perfect location in our small town. The year 2013, I opened in October, which is the start of the crazy holiday season. It all came flooding back like riding a bike! I was back in my happy place now with the support of my children. We won Best Pie that year, voted by the community. Off to a great start.

Then, the following spring, I started holding High Tea parties in front of the bakery on weekends, as if I was not busy enough. They were so popular that I decided to find a bigger location to open a legit Tea Room. Turns out there was an open space in the little vintage strip center the bakery was in. Perfect! It had been a very famous bar in its day but was now sitting all boarded up and in bad shape for two years. I worked with the owners and got a great lease as I was going to do all the work needed to transform the space into an elegant Tea Room. It took eight months of steady work to get it ready for customer use. My oldest daughter agreed to be the manager as I needed to stay with the bakery as head baker, and the tea room was only two doors away. What a wonderful addition the tea room was for the community. We were able to make all the food at the bakery and deliver it to the Tea Room hot and fresh. The space next to the tea room came available, so I signed another lease to put in a gift shop for the tea room. You know, hats, tea sets, loose-leaf teas, all the fun stuff ladies love. We were having a blast being part of so many guest's life celebrations.

Between the Tea Room and bakery was a very ticky large thrift store. Well, you guessed it. I signed a lease of that space once the thrift shop vacated. This space was in very bad condition and also took eight months to get ready. Once finished, it looked like a whole new shopping center as I now leased four of the six center spaces. It was a huge neighborhood improvement. I opened a large consignment and retail shop with great reviews. Now, I'm starting to get tired! Work work work...what have I created? I was asked to open another bakery for a new builder coming to town and wanted my business as their anchor. I declined.

Then, 2020 came!! Three of my four businesses were closed for COVID-19. The bakery was still open as it was considered an essential business. That little bakery carried all the other three businesses. I was able to pay the rent, but I had no income from them. These were hard times. I took the opportunity to make some improvements in the tea room so that when we were able to re-open, it had a feel of fresh and new. By the time I was able to bring guests back to the Tea Room, it came with many new challenges that we learned to embrace.

My daughter also got married to the love of her life in 2020, which gave us all a happy focus, not just the dreary covid sh*t. And, of course, she and her husband wanted to start a family. So, the more I thought about it, I was tired, getting older, and my other two children were just out of university. Time to make a change. Boy, did I.

I decided to sell all my businesses and my home and move to Porto, Portugal! I finished out the year and put the bakery up for sale. Within six months, the bakery had a new owner. I then listed the Tea Room and Gift Shop and, within another six months, had a new owner. Last was the Urban Barn shop, and that sold in three weeks. Now that all the businesses were sold, I put my home on the market. Selling it took a long eight months, and you know it was harder to sell my home of 20 years than the businesses. I had basically sold everything I had! Ready to move to Porto. I put my car and the few precious items in storage and headed to Porto, Portugal. My plan was to stay in Porto for one month, moving to different areas in the city each week to determine which area I would reside in. I fell in love with the slower lifestyle, the beauty of the city, the history, the food, the climate, the coast, and, of course, the people. I flew back to California after one glorious month to wrap up my affairs, sell my car, and say my goodbyes. Then God called me and said, "Go to Oregon and help your sister." What? Does my sister need help? Yep, go help your sister. So, I called my sister to ask if I could come to stay with her for one month to help her with any project she might have in the works. Turns out she had plenty. Once here in Enterprise, Oregon, I fell in love again!

The beauty of northeastern Oregon is breathtaking. So much of it reminds me of life in Portugal without the ocean. So, I decided to move here for a while and get to know the area and people better. And, of course, the entrepreneur in me has decided to open a Home Lifestyle Boutique.

Life has been such an amazing journey for me; I so look forward to all my future endeavors.

It is very important to me to follow my passions. For me, this has been achieved by meditating and through prayer. It has been necessary to listen to my inner voice in quiet moments to reflect on my future goals and to learn from my past. But the most important is to be present now.

I've learned gratitude, and that has made all the difference!

Terrie Green

Natasha Coughlan

Serial Entrepreneur, Investor & Wellness Advocate

https://www.linkedin.com/in/natasha-coughlan-10680b57/
https://www.facebook.com/natasha.coughlan
https://www.instagram.com/rugbymum_of_boys/
http://my-meals.com.au/
https://natashacoughlan.com/

Natasha Coughlan is an award-winning entrepreneur, business coach, and wellness advocate with a passion for empowering women to thrive in both life and business. As the founder of The Flourish Formula, a holistic health and wellness program, she helps women harness the power of mindset, nutrition, and self-care to achieve their personal and professional goals. Natasha also leads Meal Machines, a Tasmanian-based business dedicated to delivering nutritious, chef-crafted meals to NDIS participants, seniors, and busy individuals. Her mission is to revolutionize the way people approach health by making nutritious, delicious meals accessible to everyone. With a background in nutrition, exercise physiology, and business strategy, Natasha combines her expertise to guide others in creating balanced, fulfilled lives. Known for her authenticity, she's committed to helping individuals and businesses achieve long-lasting success.

Reflections of Strength:
From Self-Doubt to Empowerment

By Natasha Coughlan

Looking at myself in the mirror, I see words scrawled in whiteboard marker: "I am worthy, I am amazing, I am loved, I am liked." Every time I step into the bathroom, those words hit me hard. For as long as I can remember, I've wrestled with self-doubt and a deep-seated lack of self-love. Maybe it's the echoes of childhood trauma, or the toxic relationships and relentless bullying I endured. Maybe it's the way society told us that women are meant to be poor and reliant on a man—destined to be homemakers, child-bearers living under the protection of our husbands.

Growing up, I was caught between two worlds. My stepdad held old-school views that women were limited in what they could achieve, while my mum's life told a different story—one of struggle as a single mum, facing money problems, abuse, and the never-ending cycle of power imbalances. Watching her fight every day to make ends meet, I felt the weight of those expectations. I vowed early on that I wouldn't let those narratives define me.

I craved something more. I wanted to be present in my children's lives, to give them every chance to thrive, but I also knew that if I didn't keep growing, learning, and chasing new adventures, I'd never truly be fulfilled. For years, my husband and I played our parts in a traditional setup—he focused on his career as the main breadwinner while I poured my heart into raising our kids. But when the kids got older, I carved out my own space to build financial stability and to contribute in my own right.

The journey wasn't easy. Every entrepreneur knows that the road is littered with setbacks, and my path was no different. I've faced business failures, long nights filled with anxiety, and the constant battle with imposter syndrome that made me question whether I was enough. Even now, as I run an empire of businesses, self-doubt is an unwelcome companion. Yet, every stumble taught me a lesson and every setback became a stepping stone towards growth.

Back in Australia, schools rarely teach you about obligation, purpose, mission, vision, or value. It was a mentor who opened my eyes to the power of holding onto these principles, and I grabbed them with both hands. They became my anchor on the toughest days, reminding me why I do what I do and fueling my drive to keep pushing forward.

My mission now is clear—to empower other women to achieve financial independence. I believe that when you can stand on your own two feet, everything changes. The quality of the people around you, the respect you command, and the standards you set for yourself all rise. When you know your worth and no longer have to depend on someone for survival, you begin to expect more from life, and you simply won't settle for less.

Every time I stand before that mirror, reciting those affirmations, I'm reminded that I'm still a work in progress. I still battle self-doubt, but I also celebrate every win—big or small. My journey from a young woman who struggled to see her own value to an entrepreneur, a mum, and a wife with a growing empire is far from over. Each day brings a new chapter, a fresh challenge, and another chance to embrace my worth, inspire those around me, and build a legacy of strength, resilience, and unwavering belief in the power of a woman. Because in the end, it's not about never feeling doubt—it's about learning to thrive in spite of it.

Jewels Lamm

Founder of InBody
Rewire For Love & Connection

https://www.facebook.com/zinanjewel
https://www.instagram.com/inbody_with_jewels/
https://www.jewelcoaching.com
https://www.jewelcoaching.com/pages/work-with-me/copy-h-e-a-r-t-connect-session

Jewels Lamm is a Mastery Method Certified coach, Somatics Practitioner, and the visionary founder of InBody. Through this system, she facilitates a healing journey of the heart to help her clients rewire their nervous system for love and connection, break free from cycles of overwhelm, overthinking and overachieving and turn their heartaches into growth. Her signature 1:1 coaching program, Heal The Way You Love, is designed for ambitious women and brilliant leaders who are ready to create a thriving life with ease, joy, and love. With a masters in Organizational Communication and Leadership, Jewels has spent twenty years as a creative entrepreneur. From restaurant franchise owner, to yoga teacher, to wellness coach, she believes entrepreneurship is a spiritual journey of opening her heart for healing and loving herself to success and freedom! She is based in Cincinnati, Ohio. When she's not coaching, you'll find her traveling, writing, and building meaningful connections with like-minded women.

Formula For Worthiness

By Jewels Lamm

Wouldn't it be awesome to have a formula, a manual,
for worthiness in life, relationships, and business?

In math, we know that two plus two equals four. In understanding that, we know what to do, which feels very comfortable. Our minds like "black and white" thinking and a clear pathway.

When you have a question, imagine if you could open a page of your life manual and find an answer. One that tells you what to do and which pathway to follow. This feels "right" for our human mind, which likes reassurance.

I invite you to take a moment to exercise your imagination.
Close your eyes and imagine finding the answer
To your question about worthiness...
What's coming up for you?
I would love to know.

But what if we already have a formula built in us?
It is not so straightforward! It's not logical!
It's kind of hidden!
You may already be looking for it but in the "wrong" places.

For most of my life, I felt like something was missing in me.
I was broken.
Like something was wrong with me.
I felt disconnected despite my accomplishments.
This unconscious state of my being fueled my actions with doing more to be "enough" and "worthy."

Does that feel familiar to you? I feel you!

My heart was whispering. In pain. Closed.

I came to realize that I had a deep belief that I was not worthy as I was.

I was not good enough unless I was:

- Smart, so I pursued degrees, certifications, books, and courses
- Pretty, so I chased various diets and exercises
- Successful, so I started various businesses
- Perfect, so I created "sophisticated" coping strategies to avoid making mistakes

This list can go on.

I invite you to reflect on your journey and write your list.

Now, let's celebrate that part of us that knows how to get stuff done so that we can feel "good enough" but only for the moment. Yet the feeling based on this pathway does not last long. At that time, I did not know that I was following the formula that was based on the "false" premise of the logical mind that wanted to create "two plus two equals four" scenarios.

Does it mean all my efforts were wasted?
No, they were contributing to my awakening and realizing this one important wisdom.

Are you ready for it?

The wisdom is: You cannot solve an **inner perceptual issue with an outer solution.**

The inner perceptual issue is: I feel unworthy and/or not enough!
What we feel is a state of our inner being that consists of a collection of thoughts and perceptions we acquire through our life experiences.

The outer solution states that if I change something outside of me, then the inside me will change. It works in math but in complex and multidimensional humans, it is a false and distorted formula that many of us default to and continue getting stuck and delaying our healing in feeling the void.

Perhaps this is where you are—feeling exhausted, burnt out, unfulfilled, disconnected, and lacking joy despite your accomplishments, achievements, and successes. You keep doing the "right" thing. You "rescue" people in your life. You are known to be smart, a go-getter, ambitious, and strong, but deep inside, you feel lost and confused about yourself and life.

My clients often say: "My life is pretty good. I have everything I worked for. I should be feeling grateful and happy."
"What's wrong with me?" they ask next.

This question led me on my journey.
I welcome you to the world of curiosity, exploration, imagination, abundance, love, and joy that you've always wanted to experience. Here, your "not good enough" part, essentially a product of a deep wound of unworthiness, will receive what she desires.

Do you know what your "not good enough" part really wants?
Take a moment to feel her. Place your hands on your heart, breathe into your heart, and connect with the energy of feeling "not good enough." If it feels scary or awkward, it's ok. Perhaps it is your first moment to actually feel her instead of running away and avoiding the void.
She is yearning for your love and attention!
Are you connecting with that part of you?
What are you feeling? Crying? Most people cry! All of it is welcome!

When I connected with my "not good enough" for the first time, I cried too.
Then...
I let her talk and listened so she felt heard.
I held space for her in my heart, and she felt held.

I felt her through my heart, and she felt that.
I hugged her, and she received my hug.

This was my first point of connecting and coming home to my True Self through the power of love.

All that time, while I was "earning" my worth outside of me, my "not good enough" wanted to feel loved—seen, felt, heard, held, and hugged. True love is unconditional, leading us back to who we are—WHOLE. As we learn to accept all parts of ourselves through the prism of unconditional energy of love, we learn to take our power back.

Love has no agenda.
Love is the infinite energy of the Divine Creation that created us.
The sooner we realize and accept our Divine Creation, the sooner we stop our chase to prove and earn our worth. We can direct this energy to create life, relationships, and business from the energy and Spirit of Love that is within and in the Divine Creation.

It is not about doing more. It is about accepting and loving who you already are.
You are complete as you are, and YOU CAN EXPAND.
Accepting the gift of being here is the journey of an awakened heart that chooses a path of Love, a path of least resistance.

Welcome home!
You are Love!
Open your heart so it will open you to the Love that you are.

The formula is not 2+2=4!
The formula is your heart—your portal for *feeling* and *healing* all the heart wounds so you heal the way you love. You are here to experience and learn unconditional Love and share a gift of True Self!

Choose Love, and Love Always Chooses You!
The Divine Creation is Love!

The Divine Creator is Love that Loves!
Love is always here and available.
It does not come and go.
What comes and goes is our awareness of love.

Awareness is a skill I invite you to start practicing, so you can always shift back to love.

It is never about not experiencing feeling unworthy or "not good enough" in our human life; it is about coming back to Love as we integrate our human experiences with and from the Spirit of Love.

How do you feel about this formula?

If you were like me back then, you would feel triggered and resentful of Love!

It is totally normal. I see you! I feel you! I accept you!

You can continue doing what you've been doing—outsourcing love, hoping that time will heal your wounds and one day you will feel worthy and enough.

Or

You can allow your heart to lead your journey to your Radiant You and heal your heart wounds as you experience the journey of life.

Worthy or Not Worthy was never your real question.

Your real question was always: Loved or Not Loved!

Your mind questioned love because it established conditions for Love.

Love Has No Conditions!

You are unconditionally loved! Your job is to:

Receive the gift of unconditional love!

Accept all parts of yourself!

Be the Spirit of Love!

You are not separate, but you are a part of the WHOLE.

Your loving, radiant heart is a gift to this world.

Your healing heart contributes to the WHOLE healing!

Take care of your heart and you contribute to taking care of the WHOLE world!

The WHOLE world is craving for Love!

Kathryn Garcia

Founder of Sydney Events Things To Do
Event Organiser

https://www.linkedin.com/in/kathryn-g-0815aa121/
https://www.facebook.com/groups/1791542374484117
https://www.instagram.com/kathgarcia1
https://www.sydneyeventsthingstodo.com/
https://www.kathryn-garcia.com/

Kathryn Garcia is a dynamic and passionate event organiser with two decades of experience in the industry. Since 2003, she has honed her expertise, transitioning from frontline customer service roles to mastering the complexities of event management. Kathryn is not only a seasoned Brand Ambassador but also a strategic leader with a proven track record in consumer services, promotions, sales, and team management. As the visionary Founder of Sydney Events Things To Do, she continues to innovate and elevate the events landscape, creating memorable experiences that resonate with both brands and audiences alike. Kathryn is also a graduate from Western Sydney University, where she completed her Bachelor of Arts Communications degree with a major in Media in 2005. She has organised dynamic and engaging events for a diverse array of organisations. Significant events such as: International Women's Day High Tea, Breed Australia, Filipino Expo, and Christian Speed Dating.

Finding Confidence:
My Path to Self-Worth and Resilience

By Kathryn Garcia

Hi, my name is Kathryn Garcia. My purpose for sharing my story in this book is for my narrative to be the spark that ignites someone else's journey to realising their full potential and to inspire women all over the world that they can achieve whatever they set their heart and mind on. I will take you on a journey through how I became a confident and resilient woman, sharing the hardships I faced and how I overcame them.

It all started way back in my childhood days. Ever since I was a child, I was shy. I remember in kindergarten, I won an award. I can't remember what that award was, but when the teacher called out my name, I didn't want to stand up and receive the award. I was so shy to be recognised amongst my peers. When I stood up to collect my award, I was so nervous. At that moment, my confidence was low. Throughout primary and high school, I never felt confident in myself. That was due to not being pretty enough. Having pimples on my face, having braces and wearing glasses. Plus, having thick curly hair, I was teased about it. This impacted my confidence hugely in the way I presented myself to people. I wished I was pretty back then. However, I wasn't. My true beauty only showed after finishing university. I now have straight teeth. I chemically straighten my hair as I don't like having curly hair, and I also wear contact lenses. I now feel confident in my physical appearance. It was important for me to feel confident in my physical appearance, plus be confident in pursuing my dreams.

My other challenge that I didn't feel 100% perfect in my confidence was my public speaking. I don't like doing presentations. In school and at university, I also struggled to be confident in this area. It was not easy for me. Still, to this day, I don't enjoy it. However, I have challenged myself to conquer my fear of public speaking. In the past I would get an MC and write them notes to read at my events. It wasn't until I started organising and hosting Christian Speed Dating events in 2023 that I decided to face that fear head-on. I give myself a few days before the event to practise my speech. I still read my notes; however, I feel more secure and confident that I have memorised most of the information.

Most significantly, I have learnt that my worth is not dependent on the words or the opinions of others. This understanding became especially clear when I resigned from a job in the past due to its toxic work environment. After that, I couldn't find a job, and no one wanted to hire me. I didn't know what to do with my life. I was at the lowest point in my life and felt worthless. I didn't know what to do next. I decided I no longer wanted to work in a toxic environment or be mistreated in any job. I always wanted to start my own business ever since high school. So, I took the plunge and started my own business. I like being my own boss. I was happy with the flexibility it gave, having to not report to a boss and working my own hours. When I look back at that bad work experience, God was redirecting me to a better path. For me to feel happy and believe in myself that I was going to be someone one day and all the people who didn't believe in me would realise that they underestimated my potential to become successful and to inspire others. Plus, proving to myself that I am strong when things seem to fall apart and that I am made to do something more.

As a perfectionist, I've always felt the need to have everything just right. This can be a positive trait but also a setback. Please don't let others take advantage of you in any way, and have confidence in your professional abilities. I now know my worth, my value, what I can offer and not to accept less than what I deserve.

I have also realised that your past doesn't define your future. I am a living testimony of it. No matter how broken you feel in life, you can always change your destiny. Don't believe in people who say you will never make it, your business will never be successful, you're not smart enough, you're stupid, etc. You have the capacity to change how you want your life to become. Dream big and never think you can't attain your goals. I have gone through this myself, and I decided to think positively. In pursuing my dreams, I have manifested several things in my life that I never imagined could be possible. I was manifesting to be on the front cover of a magazine. I created mock-up magazine front covers and framed them in my bedroom. Every day, I looked at it. There was an opportunity that finally came to be on the front cover of a magazine. I went for it, and my dream took two years to manifest this goal. Finally, I am being recognised for my work as an event organiser. Never dim your light in the world. I know some people may feel jealous of your success. It is your light that they are afraid of. Don't give up.

I've faced moments where I had to demonstrate my true worth, particularly in romantic relationships. If someone leaves your life without recognising your value, let them go. Their departure doesn't diminish your lovability or worthiness—it reflects their own unresolved issues. The right person will see your worth, respect you, and never make the mistake of overlooking you. Remember, self-love is paramount. Love yourself with confidence. You are already complete on your own, and by loving yourself with high standards, you will naturally attract the person who truly deserves you.

My final note for all you readers is to know your worth and be resilient. By empowering yourself, you also empower other women to rise above and gain confidence. Whatever challenges you experience in your life, know that you can handle any task, no matter how big or small it is. Thought and action are powerful forces. Combine them together toward a common purpose and truly anything can happen. I believe everything in life happens for our growth, not against us. Life has the potential to offer far more than we can ever imagine. All it takes is recognising that you are destined for something greater.

Hunyah Irfan

Hunyah Travels
Content Creator

https://ca.linkedin.com/in/hunyah-irfan-blogger351
https://www.facebook.com/OfficialHunyahTravels
https://www.instagram.com/officalhunyahtravels
https://www.youtube.com/@officalhunyahtravels1

Hunyah Irfan is a content creator with a community development background. Hunyah currently facilite at Western University for Disabled Arts. Hunyah also currently facilitates with Camh University of Toronto CACHE Program. Hunyah competes in online pageants about 5 years now and ongoing. Hunyah also a spoken word artist.

The Worthy Content Creator

By Hunyah Irfan

Hi, my name is Hunyah Irfan. As you know, I'm a content creator. You may have seen Hunyah Travels on social media. I do food reviews, travel, and a lot more.

Being a content creator is great but being a worthy content creator is where you know to be a content creator without any conflicts. I'm going to share my experience and tips on being a worthy content creator.

Topics in the list are:

1. Avoid tough issues
2. Follow content creator rules
3. Don't get people to start stories about yourself

Avoid Tough Issues

Being a content creator is good. But when it comes to global issues, that is something to be careful.

Sometimes, I have seen other content creators put things like this is the political issue going in the world or somewhere.

That is good. But on the other side then, people will make terrible comments about your views.

As a content creator myself, I avoid this for a reason.

1. You don't want to get involved in this; that is for the government, leave it there
2. That can ruin your content creator career
3. You don't know what are the consequences of it

When you do share your views about politics, that is one thing not to get involved. Everyone has different views. People can find this being offensive.

Also, keep your views to yourself.

You don't want to cause more problems if there is some new rule.

For example, a few years ago in Ontario, someone started a truck post that eventually led to more problems. Whether the person was an influencer or not, I don't know.

But it's better not to get involved in it.

Plus, with elections happening this year in a few months.

It's better to keep quiet about it.

Giving your views about politics as a content creator can ruin your career too.

That is because anything can come. Going into politics may ruin your career as a content creator.

Also, you don't want people on your door asking you why do this review and support this MP, for example.

It's best to avoid it.

In my opinion, talk about common things but avoid topics like that.

Journalists, I understand there are some who talk like that.

But avoiding this would be good for a content creator.

Follow Content Creator Rules

If you are a content creator who does collaborations with different companies. Then, you have to follow each company's rules.

For example, if you are doing a collaboration with a makeup brand and doing content creation, then you have to follow the makeup company's influencer rules and do your content creation accordingly.

That is because if you don't follow that collaborative company's rules, you can lose your contract as well.

The point is just to collaborate: say yes, listen, and do the work.

Always wait for your next steps.

I suggest keeping quiet because, after the first task, you will get more projects to work on.

Also, try not to ask too many questions because that has happened to me several times.

You want to avoid that as much as possible.

The point is a common saying, "Just keep quiet and do the work."

If you are going to tell the person you support a certain team, then it could affect your work.

You have to go with the company that said it is.

Also, don't always look for money in every collaboration.

Sometimes, other collaborators are new companies that are also looking into paid options.

Being a content creator still requires you to have a second and full-time job.

Being a full-time content creator takes time.

Also, sometimes there can be fraud companies so don't rely on the paid ones.

Being a volunteer model is good too.

In my opinion, you get the experience as well.

Be careful what you sign up for and read everything.

That is because you should know what you are signing up for; that is important for any program.

Don't Get People to Start Stories about Yourself

As a content creator, there are always going to be people who will bully you. I have experienced a lot in the last six years of being a content creator now.

I have had family members like that, friends, and former workplaces as well.

You can either be a content creator who doesn't have self-respect or be a content creator who does things gracefully.

I know this one girl my age who dressed like a leopard just for followers. This girl is a content creator, too, and she also calls herself an artist.

In my opinion, I'm a content creator as well, but I would not dress like a leopard just to call myself a content creator.

I do my content creation gracefully.

If it's an actress dressing like that, I understand. But someone out of nowhere dressing like that, then you have to see which type of content creator you would like to be.

Also, if you are doing something positive as a content creator and then you hear rumors from others.

That is jealousy in many ways.

One thing I have been told whenever I do something, even content creation, is don't compare.

The minute the other content creator, for example, the one dressed like a leopard, spread a rumor about me, that is where her jealousy begins.

Did I react to it? I tried to avoid it and just blocked that girl from my social media.

Do reels and everything, but do it gracefully.

Avoid people who are jealous of your success.

These are my tips on being a worthy content creator. I hope you will find my tips helpful.

Lovely LaGuerre

Pure Heavenly Hair and Beauty Boutique
Wealth Creator, Best Selling Author &
Strategies Coach To Thrive In Life and Business

https://www.linkedin.com/in/lovelylaguerre/
https://m.facebook.com/pureheavenlyhairboutique
https://www.instagram.com/pureheavenlyhair
https://www.lovelyinspireyou.com/
http://www.pureheavenlyhair.com/
https://lovelysellsvegas.com/

MEET Lovely LaGuerre,

FOUNDER. CEO

Lovely LaGuerre is a Wealth Creator, Amazon Best Time Seller, International Bestselling Author, Commercial and Luxury Professional Real Estate, Transformational Coach On How To Thrive In Life and Business. A visionary in her own right, with an unwavering passion to inspire and empowering others.

Lovely LaGuerre is also, the driving force behind Pure Heavenly Hair and Beauty Boutique, where luxury and beauty converge.

Whether you're ready for a glamorous night out or just want to elevate your everyday look, Pure Heavenly Beauty is here to help you shine. Discover your next go-to beauty staple and transform your beauty routine today!

Explore the elegance, embrace the empowerment. Join the Pure Heavenly Beauty community at www.PureHeavenlyHair.com.

Explore the elegance, embrace the empowerment. Join the Pure Heavenly Beauty community at www.PureHeavenlyHair.com.

"The Path To Success Varies For Each Individual.
However, Becoming A True Successful Leader Requires Unwavering Commitment, Wholehearted Dedication, And The Ability To Acknowledge And Celebrate The Success Of Others."

~ Lovely LaGuerre ~

The Echo in Her Silence: Finding Strength in the Journey to Self-Worth

By Lovely LaGuerre

INTRODUCTION

In the depths of every woman's heart lies an unshakeable truth – a truth that often whispers before it roars, that builds its strength in moments of solitude before emerging into the light. I write these words not from a place of arrival, but from a space of continuous growth and discovery. This journey of understanding my worth hasn't been a straight path illuminated by constant clarity; instead, it's been a profound exploration of what it means to stand firmly in one's power while remaining open to evolution. Every day, I witness women around me questioning their value, measuring their worth against society's ever-shifting standards, and sometimes losing sight of their innate power in the chaos of daily life. But I've discovered that true worth isn't found in the noise of external validation – it's uncovered in the quiet moments when we choose to listen to our inner voice, when we dare to believe in our capacity to create change, and when we embrace every aspect of our journey with unwavering authenticity.

CHAPTER 1:
THE POWER WITHIN

> *"The moment you doubt whether you can fly,*
> *you cease forever to be able to do it."* – J.M. Barrie

I've learned that power doesn't always roar. Sometimes, it whispers, and sometimes, it's found in absolute silence. Standing in my truth required me to first understand that the volume of my voice doesn't measure my worth but the steadiness of my resolve. Every morning, I choose to embrace my strength, not because others expect it of me, but because I've discovered that true power flows from self-acceptance.

The world often tells us to be louder, to compete harder, and to push further. But I've discovered that real strength lies in knowing when to stand still, when to listen to that quiet voice inside that says, *You are enough.* This isn't about proving anything to anyone else – it's about proving to myself that I can weather any storm without losing my essence.

CHAPTER 2:
EMBRACING THE SYMPHONY OF ROLES

I wear different hats not because I have to, but because I choose to. Each role I embrace adds another layer to my identity, creating a complex harmony of responsibilities that I orchestrate with pride. Some days, I'm the executive making crucial decisions; other days, I'm the mentor guiding others toward their light. These roles aren't burdens – they're opportunities to express different facets of my strength.

The key isn't in perfecting each role, but in understanding that together, they form the fullness of who I am. When one role demands more attention, I adjust the others accordingly, like a skilled conductor leading an orchestra. This ability to pivot isn't a sign of inconsistency; it's a testament to my adaptability and resilience.

CHAPTER 3:
THE ART OF CONSISTENT EVOLUTION

Consistency isn't about doing the same things repeatedly – it's about maintaining an unwavering commitment to my values while evolving my approach. I've learned that staying on course doesn't mean following a straight line. Sometimes, the path winds and turns, but my destination remains clear.

Every morning, I recommit to my purpose, even when the path ahead seems unclear. This daily renewal of my commitment keeps me anchored when circumstances try to pull me off course. It's not about rigid adherence to plans; it's about flexible loyalty to purpose.

CHAPTER 4:
CELEBRATING EVERY STEP

"Success is not final, failure is not fatal: it is the courage to continue that counts." – Winston Churchill

I've redefined what celebration means to me. It's not just about the big wins or the obvious successes – it's about honoring every step of the journey. When I fall, I celebrate the courage it took to try. When I succeed, I celebrate not just the achievement but the persistence that made it possible.

My failures aren't setbacks; they're stepping stones. Each one teaches me something valuable about my strength, my resilience, and my capacity to rise again. I've learned to embrace these moments with grace, understanding that they're essential parts of my growth story.

CHAPTER 5:
THE FIRE THAT DRIVES

Purpose isn't just a destination – it's the fire that keeps me moving forward even when the path grows dark. I've discovered that passion isn't always a loud, consuming flame. Sometimes it's a steady ember that quietly fuels every decision, every action, every step forward.

My driving force comes from a deep understanding that my success isn't just about me. It's about creating ripples of positive change that extend far beyond my immediate reach. This understanding transforms ordinary tasks into meaningful actions, each one aligned with my greater purpose.

CHAPTER 6:
INSPIRING THROUGH AUTHENTICITY

I've learned that the most powerful way to inspire others is to live authentically in my truth. When I embrace my journey – challenges and all – I create space for others to do the same. This isn't about presenting a perfect image; it's about showing the beauty in being real, being human, and being unafraid to grow.

My story becomes a permission slip for others to embrace their journeys. By celebrating my failures alongside my successes, I demonstrate that worth isn't tied to perfection – it's tied to authenticity and the courage to keep moving forward.

CHAPTER 7:
THE QUIET REVOLUTION

"In a gentle way, you can shake the world." – Mahatma Gandhi

I'm leading a quiet revolution – one that begins within and ripples outward through every life I touch. My determination isn't about making noise; it's about making an impact. My zest for life isn't measured in grand gestures but in the consistent choice to show up fully, authentically, and purposefully each day.

This revolution is built on the understanding that true power often works silently, transforming lives not through force, but through inspiration. It's about creating change not by demanding attention, but by commanding respect through actions aligned with values.

CHAPTER 8:
STANDING IN UNSHAKEABLE TRUTH

I've discovered that standing in my power isn't about being immovable – it's about being intentionally present in every moment. When the noise of the world grows loud, I don't need to shout above it. Instead, I center myself in my truth, letting my actions speak with clarity and purpose.

My worth isn't determined by external validation or others' expectations. It's an internal flame that I've learned to tend carefully, protecting it from the winds of doubt while allowing it to grow stronger with each challenge I face.

CHAPTER 9:
THE LEGACY OF RESILIENCE

"The most difficult thing is the decision to act, the rest is merely tenacity." – Amelia Earhart

Every step I take, every challenge I overcome, and every success I achieve becomes part of a larger legacy. This legacy isn't built on perfection – it's built on persistence. It's created through the quiet moments when I choose to keep going, even when the path ahead seems uncertain.

My unwavering determination comes from understanding that each moment is an opportunity to demonstrate the power of resilience. This isn't just about achieving personal success; it's about showing others what's possible when you refuse to let circumstances define your worth.

CONCLUSION:
THE CONTINUING JOURNEY

The journey to knowing your worth never truly ends – it evolves, deepens, and transforms with each passing day. I've learned that true strength lies not in never falling, but in rising every time life knocks you down. My worth isn't measured by the obstacles I face, but by the courage and grace with which I face them.

As I continue to stand in my power, wear my many hats with pride, and maintain my course with unwavering determination, I remember that my journey isn't just about me. It's about creating a path that others can follow, showing them that it's possible to be both strong and gentle, both determined and flexible, both successful and authentically human.

The echo in my silence speaks volumes about who I am and what I stand for. It carries the wisdom of every lesson learned, the strength of every challenge overcome, and the promise of every dream yet to be achieved. This is what it means to know your worth – not as a destination to reach, but as a truth to live every single day.

JOIN THE MOVEMENT!
#BAUW

Becoming An Unstoppable Woman
With She Rises Studios

She Rises Studios was founded by Hanna Olivas and Adriana Luna Carlos, the mother-daughter duo, in mid-2020 as they saw a need to help empower women worldwide. They are the podcast hosts of the *She Rises Studios Podcast* and Amazon best-selling authors and motivational speakers who travel the world. Hanna and Adriana are the movement creators of #BAUW - Becoming An Unstoppable Woman: The movement has been created to universally impact women of all ages, at whatever stage of life, to overcome insecurities, and adversities, and develop an unstoppable mindset. She Rises Studios educates, celebrates, and empowers women globally.

Looking to Join Us in our Next Anthology or Publish YOUR Own?

She Rises Studios Publishing offers full-service publishing, marketing, book tour, and campaign services. For more information, contact info@sherisesstudios.com

We are always looking for women who want to share their stories and expertise and feature their businesses on our podcasts, in our books, and in our magazines.

SEE WHAT WE DO

OUR PODCAST

OUR BOOKS

OUR SERVICES

Be featured in the Becoming An Unstoppable Woman magazine, published in 13 countries and sold in all major retailers. Get the visibility you need to LEVEL UP in your business!

Have your own TV show streamed across major platforms like Roku TV, Amazon Fire Stick, Apple TV and more!

Learn to leverage your expertise. Build your online presence and grow your audience with FENIX TV.
https://fenixtv.sherisesstudios.com/

Visit www.SheRisesStudios.com to see how YOU can join the #BAUW movement and help your community to achieve the UNSTOPPABLE mindset.

Have you checked out the *She Rises Studios Podcast?*

Find us on all MAJOR platforms: Spotify, IHeartRadio, Apple Podcasts, Google Podcasts, etc.

Looking to become a sponsor or build a partnership?

Email us at info@sherisesstudios.com

SHE RISES
STUDIOS

www.ingramcontent.com/pod-product-compliance
Lightning Source LLC
Chambersburg PA
CBHW061718120626
46550CB00003B/1283